AF250326

HEY YOU

ALSO BY THE AUTHOR

FICTION

Ghost Man

Shine

POETRY

Naked

HEY YOU

Donnelle McGee

THERA BOOKS
Turlock, California

Acknowledgments

Grateful acknowledgment is made to the editors of the following publications, in which some poems in this book first appeared, sometimes in different form.

Ginosko Literary Journal: "After the Trauma"
The Santa Clara Weekly: "A Heart Where I Will Lay My Head"
Umbrella Factory: "Steel"

Copyright

Hey You: Poems.
Copyright © 2019 by Donnelle McGee.

Cover Design: Mona Z. Kraculdy.

All rights reserved. No part of this book can be reproduced in any form by any means without written permission. Please address inquiries to the publisher:

Thera Books
1819 Empress Lane
Turlock, CA 95382

E-mail: dmcgeewriter@gmail.com

Printed in the United States of America.
ISBN: 978-0-578-44091-0
Library of Congress Control Number: 2019900190

A Thera Books First Edition

FOR

Some Place Beautiful

Open your heart, I'm coming home
But it was only fantasy

The wall was too high, as you can see

–Pink Floyd

#8A

met a woman once   watched her go crazy

   her soft   wild hazel eyes burn my belly

DOWNHILL

this spring i walk

downhill

past break of his shadow to split lies open

this spring i walk

downhill

steps sure and easy   done holding her up

TRAUMA

1.

Watched her crumble. With a glass of red wine by her side she went
    crazy. But I understand. Crazy attracts crazy. Crazy.
He first.
Then she.
Then me.

2.

Hazel eyes.   Blonde hair.   Naturally mousey.   Colored golden.
Met her on Yahoo.

3.

She met her ex on E-harmony.
He came to live with her.
No rent.
Little sex.   Departed in January.
I came to her in February.

4.

Our first day together. She and me.
Lovely as she walked down the stairs of her condo to me.
Red sweater. Peace symbol on front. Yellows, greens, gold, and
    blues.
Blue jeans on slender frame. Her eyes sun in my eyes.
Brunch at a tower.
Walk at a river. Hair put into a tight pony-tail.
I fall quickly.

Later. A movie. A bottle of Coopola. Red.
Inside her. We have begun.

The only thing is this. She never. Or. He or they both never left one
    another.

Later she will tell me that she has OCD manifested via anorexia.
There are other things too.
But shit, I got issues too. And they all came out.

5.

And I learned how to hate more fully.

HERE WITH ANAGARIKA MUNINDRA
Woodacre, CA

when all there is before us

are trees   these pines

red tint   deep greens

below white-blue sky

space to melt existence

space

to just be

DELUSIONAL

he told her he took a bullet in the stomach
a few days in a coma
fbi undercover operation

out of coma   claiming he had to be with her
couldn't live without her   she   the love of his life

only problem was this   there was never a bullet

the day i saw his picture i told her he's too weak to get shot
and so it went   his stomach untouched

STEEL

kunitz said in the layers

        i am not done with my changes

and with the golden gate before me

its arc full   steel / red / orange

bay water punching rock

i stand in faded pea coat staring at a fisherman's pole

this little man waiting for the bite

for the change in the bend of his pole before the reel in

THE MORNING AFTER THE FIRST LIE

sky pink

before

mustard hills turn green

this space between us

bleeding

BUDDHA

three

deer here   behind me

watching me   watching them

IN DEEP

told her

i'm a wonderer

whatever that meant

still i'm moving again

how i wish she would ground me

but she can't

trauma in her deep

JIMI SAW THIS TOO

i will do my best to capture this
although poetry fails us at times

>   but here it is
>   chalk moon full
>   purple blue sky

>   i get it jimi
>   purple haze soothes

SACRAMENTO

when a body breaks
all that truth
compassion
has no place to go but out
and for a minute i hear coltrane calling me in
or maybe miles
but all that is
is

KILLING US SOFTLY

lauryn hill

13

what flack call her   *L boogie*

flipping souls
words coming out of a body on fire

5 A.M. IN SACRAMENTO

here again
crossroads

hermit on path
lips pink quiver

words breaking a deep song
like lorca

perhaps words that depart body must be written first with awareness
with a heightened if not down right fearful presence of death

well then   let them come
dance numbness in them hills where summer violet petals wilt

and love
enters morning

hazel eyes and
pale flesh keeping me here

SLICES OF LOVE

Love holds
Love holds
Love holds
Love holds
Love holds
Love holds
Love holds
Love holds
Love holds
Love holds
Love holds
Love holds
Love holds
Love holds

BEAUTIFUL

i have grown tired

       of the love poem

i have grown tired

AMUART

a poem inside a poem

what would that be

a man inside his love

a woman kissing the inside of her love's soft thighs

a man letting tongue move pleasure into his love's mouth

a woman on top of her woman

a man on top of his woman

a man on top of his man

a woman on top of her man

I DON'T CARE

i turn to hold her

18

left work early

i don't care

the green of her eyes

trumps it all

tuck pride in red sheets

to be with her

i don't care

the green of her eyes

trumps it all

A HEART WHERE I WILL LAY MY HEAD

the one with violets in her lap
is eyeing me

pale hands
set softly

in purple
blooms

them hazel
eyes

seeing through me
to times where

the buckle of loss
dissipates

to let come
the burst of

blossoms
which cover

the space
between her thighs

a heart
where i

lay
my head

THERE COMES A MOMENT

when you lick your teeth and know

no one can heal you   bring you sane/full

NEBRASKA CORNFIELD

She screaming
Sunlight bathing green field yellow

This gig bringing
Bones together

Plum clouds rifting in blue sky
She screaming

This gig of a lifetime given
Swallowing sky

Cries brisk
She sways her voice

Above ripening stalks
In this Nebraska cornfield

Sitting
Unafraid

She
Screams

Come get me
I've tasted sky

—after hearing Pink Floyd's "The Great Gig in the Sky"

WHITENESS

naked as i write this after leaving her body

                                                 breathe

tell me again

                                                 breathe

inside this poem the contour of her body bends white space

                                                 breathe

but she ain't here

                                                 breathe

SPACE

When she said give her space I didn't Limbs twitch Eyes dart Heart gone Prey Surround her I have become wild Part of the craze that roams her Only later when her words sunk through was I able to let space move between us And I understand the gift she gave

TRAUMA THERAPY

tap tap taptaptap   tap   tap

on roof of my element

rain on me   door open i move

blue moon above

concrete path lighted white

throwing my hands up to endure what is

AFTER THE TRAUMA

I touch her hands and know this much

25

compassion rescues a body from chaos

and so this story goes   truth call me in   let her breathe

56 TEXTS TO NAPA

in bed with me one night

the next three with him

nearly a nervous breakdown

but i hold

still   them three nights in napa with delusion piercing my stomach

on her return she takes sick

and i come to her

in a month he will be gone   his confession slipping from his crossed
     eyes

HEY YOU

after Pink Floyd

Yellow petals around brown yolk of sunflower
That's how she came

Faded lavender petals of agapanthus
Dry and wasted is how she left

Found self face down in a mound of caine
White powder under eyes

She saying Hey you
Would you touch me

And   Hey you
Open your heart I'm coming home

When she returned
Red starred dress clinging to frail frame

I took her in my arms
Telling her Hey you

ALONE WITH NO BULLET WOUND

the sociopath-con fades in late march

blue drizzly night in sac

his lies choke him

this man confesses all

doorbell ditch

repeated calls and hang-ups

delusions his

fbi

therapist

lawyers

actors paid

he can't remember

until the end

when truth bites

the uncovering too much

another woman stalked

this sociopath-con tired of being alone

but alone he will be

watching him place six

red roses on the grave brings me to knees

one need not know particulars

RETURN

When you open the door to leave this room—

where Sasha crawls over us
her soft white fur brushing us awake

this room where our voices light darkness with
hopes of running through wild flowers in Holland —

Make sure you close it softly and return

ABOUT THE AUTHOR

Donnelle McGee is the author of the novel *Ghost Man* (Sibling Rivalry Press), the novella *Shine* (Sibling Rivalry Press), and the poetry collection *Naked* (Unbound Content). He earned his MFA from Goddard College. He is a faculty member at Mission College in Santa Clara, California. His work has appeared in *Controlled Burn, Colere, Haight Ashbury Literary Journal, Home Planet News, Iodine Poetry Journal, Permafrost, River Oak Review, The Spoon River Poetry Review,* and *Willard & Maple,* among others. His work has also been nominated for a Pushcart Prize. Donnelle lives in Turlock, California.

www.ingramcontent.com/pod-product-compliance
Lightning Source LLC
Chambersburg PA
CBHW032133050726

47590CB00008B/3080